Riel's People

Riel's People
How the Métis Lived
Maria Campbell
Illustrated by David Maclagan

Douglas & McIntyre
Vancouver

This book has been written for Nicola,
whose father gave his life to the Métis people.

Douglas & McIntyre Ltd.
1875 Welch Street
North Vancouver, British Columbia

Canadian Cataloguing in Publication Data

Campbell, Maria.
    Riel's people
(How they lived in Canada)

    ISBN 0-88894-222-2

    1. Métis* - Canada - Juvenile literature.
I. Maclagan, David, 1932-   II. Title.
III. Series.
FC109.C34   j971'.004'97   C78-002174-6
F1035.M4C34

Typesetting by Frebo Studio Limited
Design by David Maclagan
Jacket art by David Maclagan
Printed and bound in Canada by D.W. Friesen & Sons Ltd.

Contents

Sowing Grain

The Métis: Beginnings

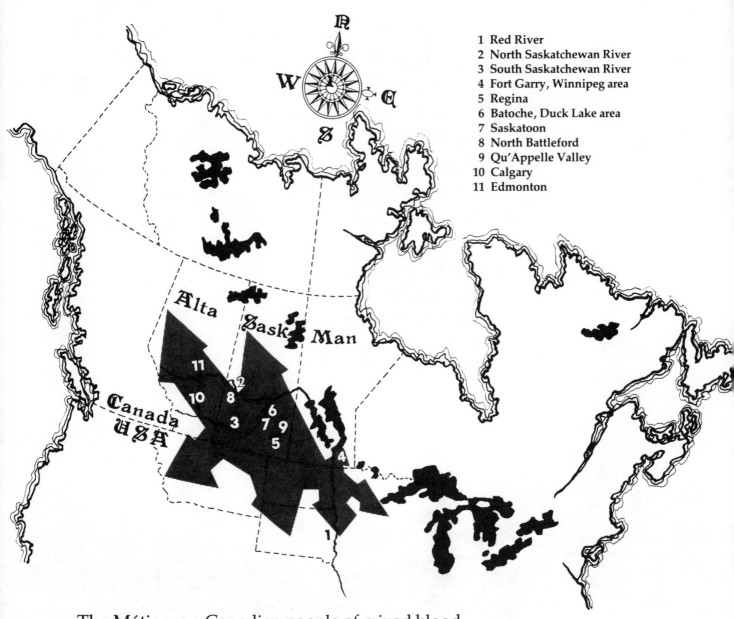

1 Red River
2 North Saskatchewan River
3 South Saskatchewan River
4 Fort Garry, Winnipeg area
5 Regina
6 Batoche, Duck Lake area
7 Saskatoon
8 North Battleford
9 Qu'Appelle Valley
10 Calgary
11 Edmonton

The Métis are a Canadian people of mixed blood, Indian and white. Three centuries ago their mothers were Indian; their fathers were the explorers and fur traders who came from Britain and France. Although they played an important role in Canadian history, they have been often ignored or misunderstood.

In Europe during the sixteenth century, well-dressed men wore high felt hats, and beaver fur made an excellent waterproof felt cloth with strong fibres that retained for years the shape and height of the hat. Fur-trading companies were formed which paid large sums of money to adventurers who would trade for beaver pelts in North America.

The white fur traders needed the Indians to trap the beaver, and so became friendly with them. Some took Indian wives, partly to help business, because an Indian wife could interpret for her husband. As well, traders who married the daughter of a chief would have the business of the chief's people and probably that of the neighbouring bands.

Their children spoke the languages of both parents, and when old enough, they too worked for the companies. So began a new and truly native work force of canoemen, traders, labourers, interpreters, and fur packers. Sometimes, becoming trappers, they competed with their Indian relatives for the furs. Some Métis children were sent to Quebec or Great Britain to be educated, and when they came back were hired as clerks by the fur companies. The fur trade expanded, and as it grew so did the Métis, who in time called themselves "The New Nation."

Beaver Hat
Métis Trapper
Beaver

Becoming a People

When the beaver became scarce in one area, the fur traders explored deeper into the continent in search of pelts. The Indians who exchanged beaver pelts for trade goods, such as guns, knives, axes, copper kettles, beads, cloth and blankets, became dependent on the fur trader and to obtain more fur they had to seek new trapping grounds. This meant invading land occupied by other tribes, and wars resulted. The Indian trappers moved north, west, and south, and the fur-trading companies and Métis followed close behind.

As the Métis grew in numbers, the Indians decreased, being killed by wars and European diseases. The Métis were not so badly affected by these diseases, probably because they had better access to the white man's medicine and perhaps because their mixed blood provided some immunity.

Trading Depot

With the increase in distances that the furs had to be carried, the canoes could not carry enough food for the travellers, so food was stocked in depots across the country. Supplying this meat became an industry for the Métis, who now outnumbered the whites. From the buffalo that they hunted they provided hides for the traders' clothing, and meat that could be sold or preserved as pemmican.

As time passed the staffs of the fur companies needed more pemmican to feed themselves and the settlers who were travelling west in increasing numbers. More and more buffalo had to be killed to meet the demand. The Indians who depended on the buffalo for their food, shelter and clothing became alarmed by the decrease in the herds, and there were many fights between the Métis and the Indians, particularly with the Sioux, in whose lands the Métis often hunted. For both Indians and Métis the loss of the buffalo meant the end of a free and independent way of life.

The early fur trade depended on the voyageurs or *coureurs de bois*. They were the men whom the fur companies hired to travel the rivers and lakes of the west in canoes — later, in the larger York boats — to carry the furs back to the trading posts. A voyage for a *coureur de bois* could be from one hundred to several thousand miles long. These expert rivermen found their way over the vast land with the aid of the stars, although they later had maps.

The voyageurs paddled sixteen to eighteen hours a day, and when they came to rapids, waterfalls, or stretches of low water they portaged, emptying the canoe and carrying it and its load around the obstacles. They had to climb rocky banks, skirt bogs and penetrate dense bush with their heavy loads. Often they were up to the waist in icy water as they loaded their canoes.

To make portages possible the cargo was packed in 90-pound bundles, two of which were carried in a sling that went around the man's forehead and hung down his back. Slightly stooped to lean into the weight and moving with a shuffling trot, the man covered half a mile in ten minutes, after which he had a short rest.

The canoe, which usually weighed 600 pounds, was made of birch bark and sealed with spruce pitch. Depending on the distance to be travelled and the size of the load, from four to ten men would man a canoe. At portages, four men carried it upside down on their shoulders while the others carried the supplies, furs and trade goods.

The voyageurs' day began at 2:00 a.m., and they paddled until breakfast around 8:00. Lunch at noon consisted of a piece of pemmican eaten while still paddling, and they continued until 9:00 p.m., when they had supper followed by a few hours sleep. Because speed was important they carried food with them; only in emergencies did they hunt and fish while travelling.

York Boat

At the end of each hour's paddling, which would cover four or five miles, they rested on their paddles and smoked a pipe. A voyage would be measured in pipes. Even today, a Métis trapper might say that his trapline is ten pipes wide and fifteen pipes long.

The York boat was developed in 1885 by a Métis, William Sinclair. It was built of wood and was 30 feet in length, 8 or more feet wide. It was cumbersome but very sturdy, and carried four times as much as a canoe. When there was a breeze and the water was smooth, sails were hoisted; otherwise ten men were needed to row it.

The voyageurs did not like the York boats because they were very heavy and could not be portaged. In shallow or difficult water they had to be pulled with long ropes from shore.

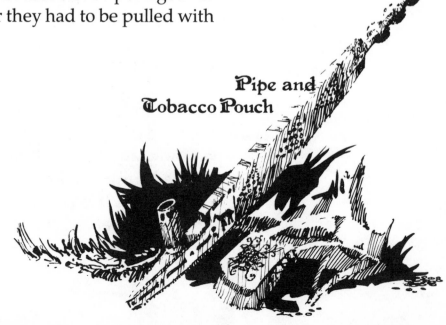

Pipe and
Tobacco Pouch

Hunting and Trapping

In the early spring hundreds of Métis families from various settlements would gather on the plains along the banks of the Assiniboine, in what is now known as Manitoba, to prepare for the annual buffalo hunt. They formed a caravan of 1,500 to 2,000 ox-driven Red River carts accompanied by hundreds of horses and many dogs. A captain and councillors would be elected to make and enforce laws so that there would be no trouble in the community. The bravest young men with the swiftest horses were chosen as scouts to ride ahead of the caravan looking for buffalo or Indian war parties. A Roman Catholic priest usually travelled with the caravan to hold mass and to bless the scouts each day.

A Métis Scout

When the captain gave the order the caravan moved off west. At night the carts were drawn into a protective circle in which the animals were corralled. Teepees were set up inside the circle. The men started fires over which the women cooked, and the evening was spent smoking and visiting, singing and dancing.

If, when on the move, the scouts spotted a war party, the carts were swung into a circle, provisions piled against them as added defences, and trenches dug for the women and children to lie in for protection. The men would wait behind the carts; no shot was fired until the captain was certain that the Indians were going to attack. The Métis were not a warring people and preferred to settle problems by talking.

When the scouts sighted buffalo, camp was made and the hunters prepared to ride. They would ensure that their elaborately decorated leather saddles and bridles were secure, their bed rolls and grub bags fastened, their bone-handled skinning knives sharp, their medicine kits of herbs and roots in their saddle bags, and their most prized possessions — their rifles — clean and working.

The most common method of hunting was called "running the buffalo." The hunters formed a long line and, when the captain gave the order, started out at a slow trot, increasing the pace until they were galloping when close to the herd. No one was allowed to shoot until the order was given. Then the horsemen galloped into the stampeding herd and began shooting the buffalo as they swept through them. They would turn their horses and run into the herd again and again until they had sufficient meat.

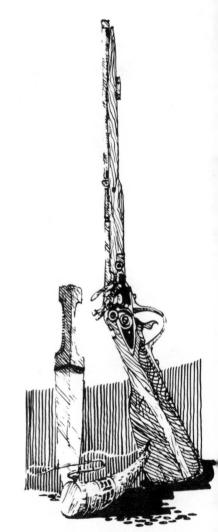

1841 Parker Trade Gun
Trade Knife
Powder Horn

Buffalo Hunters

The hunters were always in great danger. A horse could step into a gopher's burrow and stumble, throwing the rider under the hooves of the herd. A horse might be gored by a rampaging bull. Always there was the danger of stray bullets or an exploding gun.

A hunter slung his powder horn on a thong around his neck and carried six lead balls in his mouth. As he rode at top speed through the herd he poured powder into the muzzle of the gun, spat the lead ball on top of it, picked out his animal, aimed his gun at its heart, and shot it — all the while guiding his horse with his knees. It was no wonder that these men were considered among the most expert horsemen in the world, and their horses among the best trained. After the hunter had shot the buffalo he threw down beside it a piece of his clothing or a coloured cloth that would identify the kill as his.

Skinning Buffalo

When enough buffalo had been shot the women arrived to skin and quarter the carcases, which were then loaded on the carts and hauled back to camp. A feast of fresh buffalo meat was prepared, the priest conducted a service, and the successful hunt was celebrated with music and dancing. The following day, the making of pemmican would begin.

Smaller animals such as beaver, mink, otter, muskrat and lynx were snared to obtain furs for clothing. Later, when the buffalo had almost gone, the Métis trapped and sold these smaller pelts for their livelihood, using metal traps obtained from the trading posts.

Family Life

Métis families were close-knit and large, with often ten or more children and at least one grandparent. A number of families lived together in settlements and shared what they had with each other. They were loyal and very protective of one another.

The Métis were religious, the majority of them being Roman Catholic, Anglican or Methodist, but they also respected Indian taboos and beliefs. Consequently, their religion was sometimes a mixture of Indian beliefs and Christian practices, and not always what the missionaries wanted.

Rectory and Church at Batoche

They married in churches, and the celebration
that followed would go on for days, with dancing
and feasting. The whole settlement would take part,
helping with the cooking and baking for days before
the wedding.

The bride and groom wore their best clothes, and
the horses and buggy (in winter a sleigh called a
cariole) which carried the young couple to church
would be trimmed with bells and ribbons. As the
bridal couple drove to church, other family rigs
followed in a gay procession.

Most young people married because they
loved each other, though some marriages
were arranged by parents. Divorce was almost
unheard of, because it was not accepted by
the Catholic church and was frowned
upon by the other churches. If a couple
found it hard to live together, they
separated but would never marry again.

Education was respected by the Métis but it was difficult to get. Schools were far away and cost a great deal of money. Those early Métis who were educated had been trained by the church as priests, nuns or ministers, or had been sent to schools in Quebec or Great Britain by their white fathers.

In earlier years, bilingual schools were built, and staffed by nuns; one was at Red River, Manitoba, and another at Batoche, Saskatchewan. To attend such a school a Métis child had to live away from home for years. Many parents felt that the family was too important to be broken up, and kept their children with them to learn Métis skills instead of reading, writing and memorizing from books. These children learned the settlement's history from the old storytellers, whose songs and legends had been passed down through generations, and so they grew up proud of being Métis.

Violin and Concertina

The Métis loved music, and mixed traditional Indian dances with the reels and jigs of Scotland and France to create original dances such as the Red River Jig and the Duck Dance. The Scottish fiddle became the favourite instrument of the Métis, but they also played the concertina and the mouth harp, an instrument held between the teeth that produces a twanging sound. Children joined in the music-making and danced with the adults.

Little girls played with dolls of tanned hide and rags made by their grandmothers, and spent hours sewing clothes for their dolls. The men — who were fond of whittling wood — carved animals and other small figures and made whistles from red willows.

Small drums were made by
stretching skins over small hollow
logs. Boys pretended to go on buffalo
hunts with their little bows and arrows,
stick horses and wooden muzzle-loaders.

"Huntin Buff'lo"

Bringing in Firewood

The children were taught early how to survive outdoors and soon became skilled with snowshoes, toboggans and the handling of dog teams. Their games helped them to learn outdoor skills.

The men loved to dance and sing but they also liked to argue about politics. Best of all they loved to gamble, and would wager on anything. Card games could go on for days, and it was not uncommon for a man to wager everything he owned on a horse race.

Women's pleasure mostly came from sewing, visiting and conversation, and playing with their children. Sometimes they took part in the gambling games of the men, but usually they gambled among themselves. Métis women were as strong and independent as their men, and often as involved in the politics that affected their lives; however, their main role was that of keeping a good home.

Métis art was largely decorative: beadwork, silk embroidery, and the weaving of colourful cloth for sashes and shawls. There were carved or whittled wooden ornaments in the homes, and often the furniture — especially the cradles and chairs — was beautifully made.

Sod Roof

Door Hinge

Construction of a Log Cabin

Shelter

The Métis usually lived in log houses or, when travelling, in teepees like those of the plains Indians. To build a log house they sawed or chopped down straight pine trees which they peeled and dried. They notched each end of the logs with a broadaxe and fitted them together, cutting out windows and a door. Frames for the door and windows were also made from hand-hewn logs. They made hinges of leather, and for nails used wooden pegs. The roof was made of split logs and covered with sod or wood slabs like shingles.

The walls were chinked with mud plaster that had been mixed with chopped prairie grass. The windows were covered with stretched rawhide made from deerskin, which could be scraped enough to let the light in. The door was fashioned from split logs held together by wooden pegs or nails.

Axe, Draw Knife and Saw

A mud or clay fireplace with a chimney heated the interior and served for cooking. It also provided light, though candles and oil lamps were used. Pots hung over the fire: a small one for tea and a large one for stew or soup.

Tables, benches and beds were made from split logs that had been smoothed with a hand plane, a draw knife or a sharp axe. Beds were covered with buffalo robes and with blankets obtained from the trading posts.

Herbs

The walls held pegs for hanging clothes and shelves for storing dishes. There were usually many kinds of dried herbs and roots hanging from the rafters, filling the house with lovely smells. Herbs and roots were used for medicine and cooking.

Always on one wall hung a fiddle and, if the family were Roman Catholic, a crucifix. No home was complete without them.

Stables, barns and outbuildings were separate from the living quarters. Root cellars were dug under most houses to store vegetables in the winter and to keep food cool in the summer. In the winter meat was frozen and stored outside in heavy containers or placed in trees to prevent animals from eating it.

At first the outsides of cabins were not decorated, as building the shelter and obtaining food were more important, but later the Métis whitewashed their homes, usually every year.

Crucifix and Jesuit Cross

The Teepee

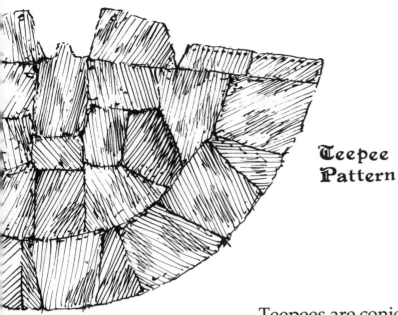

**Teepee
Pattern**

Teepees are conical tents made of buffalo hides. With neighbours helping each other the Métis erected a teepee by lashing together three poles with rawhide thongs, then raising the poles to make a tripod. The thongs which tied the poles together were long enough to reach the ground, where they were pegged like guy wires to give additional support.

Thirteen poles or more, depending on the size of teepee wanted, were leaned counterclockwise around the tripod and covered with twelve to twenty buffalo skins carefully cut and sewn together with sinew to a precise pattern. This cover was tightly drawn around the poles and then pinned with wooden pegs. Although it looked fragile, the teepee was very sturdy and could withstand the strong prairie winds.

A hole for a chimney was left at the top above the centre of the teepee, where the fire was always laid. Two poles with flaps acted as a damper to control the heat and smoke and to keep out snow. A fire pit was used on rainy days and during the winter. Otherwise cooking was done outdoors.

The floor was covered with prairie grass, and buffalo robes were laid down for sleeping on. Backrests woven from willow branches were used as chairs.

Clothing

The clothing worn by the Métis combined fashions
worn by Europeans and Indians, with perhaps more
colour and individual style. Most clothing was made
at home by the women from cloth obtained at the
trading posts or from deerskins and moosehides.

Men wore corduroy or tanned deerskin or
moosehide trousers with beaded or brightly
coloured suspenders; their shirts were of wool or
cotton in bright colours, with beaded armbands.
Sometimes they wore tanned deerskin or
moosehide shirts and jackets decorated with
beadwork. On their feet they wore woollen
stockings and beaded moosehide moccasins, and
sometimes deerskin or moosehide leggings; on their
heads, woollen caps or large broad-brimmed hats.
For warmth they wore a capote, a garment like a
modern-day parka, made from a Hudson's Bay
blanket. At the waist the capote was tied with a
bright sash, called a l'Assomption or Red River sash,
which was finger woven from wool and could be up
to twenty feet long. This sash was a most useful
article of clothing, for it was used as a belt for hauling
canoes over portages, and whenever else a rope or a
chain was needed.

Women were very style-conscious, and fashioned clothing that was attractive as well as serviceable out of whatever material was available. They wore skirts and full-sleeved colourful blouses pleated at the bodice and tucked into the skirt. Their skirts were gathered and decorated with ribbons. Sometimes they wore sashes similar to the men's.

Women's footwear was beaded moccasins and velvet or woollen leggings. High button shoes were highly prized by the women, but rare. On their heads they wore scarves or shawls.

The women wrapped a blanket about them in the winter and a shawl in the summer. Sometimes they made coats from Hudson's Bay blankets. Later, they bought their clothes ready-made in European fashions from the depots.

Children were dressed in the same style clothing as the adults. Moss-filled bags kept babies warm and comfortable.

Household Articles

Fleshing Tool
Hide Scraper
Copper Pot

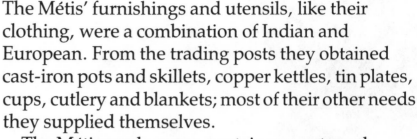

The Métis' furnishings and utensils, like their clothing, were a combination of Indian and European. From the trading posts they obtained cast-iron pots and skillets, copper kettles, tin plates, cups, cutlery and blankets; most of their other needs they supplied themselves.

The Métis made many containers, pots and storage bags from the hides of buffalo and smaller game. Rawhide (animal skin with the fur scraped off) was cut and sewn to make containers. Sometimes the Métis made cooking pots from rawhide, and to prevent the skin from collapsing when it was wet they gave it a frame of willow. A skin pot could not be placed over flames, so stones were heated in the fire and dropped into the water to make it boil.

Containers and baskets were also made from birch bark sewn with spruce roots. These were preferred over woven willow and reed baskets, which were too cumbersome when families were on the move.

To store needles, a bone of a rabbit or another small animal was hollowed out, cleaned and plugged at both ends. The stomachs of small game, when cleaned and dried, made excellent airtight bags.

Tea Cozy

Decorated Bag

Sinew, the back muscle of an animal, was commonly used for sewing. It is long and stringy and, when dried and separated, makes an excellent thread that is almost impossible to break. Glue was obtained by boiling down animals' hooves or horns to a fine paste.

For scraping the flesh and fat off hides the Métis used scrapers with stone or metal blades and fleshers made from the thigh and leg bones of animals, the edges being serrated. Needles were purchased from traders, but in early times an awl was used to pierce holes for the sinew to pass through.

Dishes could be made from hollowed-out slabs of wood, and from birch bark. Rock and stone hammers and mauls were made by grinding rocks for hours with another stone. With a maul, buffalo meat and wild berries could be pounded on a hollowed-out stone to make pemmican.

As blankets and rugs, buffalo robes were used, and when cloth scraps were available a woman could produce a quilt by making a sheet from many small pieces, sewing the sheet into a bag and stuffing it with feathers or down.

Like their sisters the plains Indian women, Métis women put colourful designs and patterns on the articles they used every day, sometimes for spiritual reasons — for they were part Indian — but most often because of their love of decoration.

Quilting

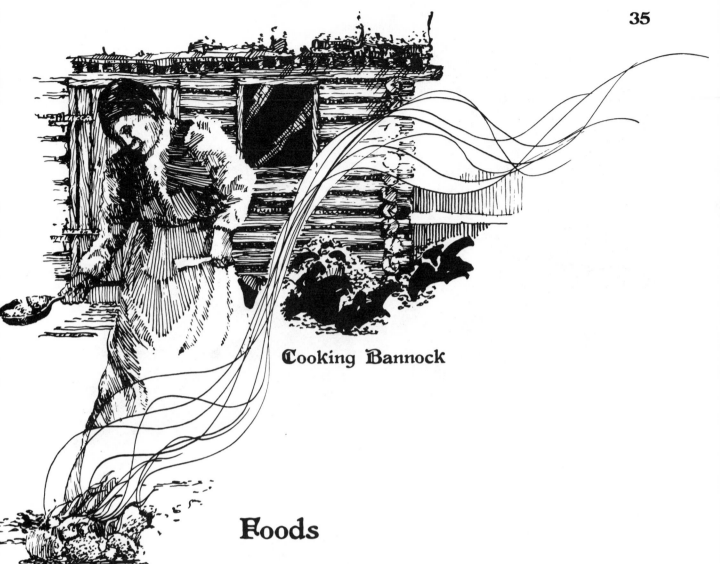

Cooking Bannock

Foods

Buffalo meat was the mainstay of the Métis diet, but the people also ate fish, antelope, moose, elk, rabbits, prairie chickens (a kind of grouse), ducks and geese. They picked berries and stored them in skin containers. Wild turnip, when peeled, dried and pounded, made an excellent flour for soup, and herbs were used for flavouring.

The Métis, being of European descent, ate the same food as most settlers. They used flour, sugar and other ingredients available from trading posts. Bannock, a traditional Scottish bread made from flour, lard and water, was baked by the Métis; outdoors it was cooked in a skillet over an open fire. Bannock kept for long periods of time and was very filling. The Métis called it *gellette*.

Drying Meat for Pemmican

Pemmican was made by cutting buffalo meat into long thin slices that were hung to dry by the sun on racks made of willows. In later years the meat was dried with a small fire burning under the rack of meat, tended by the old women and the children. If wood was not available for the fire then dried buffalo droppings were used.

When the meat was dry it was put into bags and pounded by the men and women into a fine powder which was then mixed with hot buffalo fat, cooled, and packed into airtight bags. Sometimes wild berries were added to give it flavour. Pemmican was very nourishing and filling. It kept for years without spoiling and was very easy to carry.

When the Métis lived in settlements and on farms, they planted gardens and raised livestock for food just as the white settlers did. Métis women always had tea ready and a pot of stew or soup on the fire; no one ever visited a Métis home without being offered hospitality.

Transportation

The Métis used dogs, horses and oxen to pull a variety of carts, wagons, toboggans and sleighs. Horses, obtained by trading — and sometimes by stealing — were also used for riding and for hunting.

In the winter, dogs pulled toboggans made from willow frames and covered with a wet rawhide that was shaped over the frame and left to freeze. In the spring when the rawhide thawed it was cut up for mending snowshoes and other uses.

Horses were also used to pull toboggans and the elaborate and showy carioles which were used for pleasure only. The runners of the cariole were made from birch wood that had been carefully chosen, cut, boiled and shaped. The frame was also made of birch wood, usually carved; the edges were trimmed with bright ribbons or wool woven into a braid. When the seat had been fitted in, fur robes were laid over it. With the horses' harness polished and decorated with bells and ribbons, it made a very handsome rig.

Horse and Cutter

The Métis made snowshoes from young peeled saplings that were boiled to make them pliable for shaping. Once shaped, the wood was notched and tied with rawhide thongs. The inside of the frame was woven with wet rawhide, which became taut when dry. The snowshoes were secured to the feet with rawhide thongs.

Snowshoes

The most famous Métis vehicle was the Red River cart. It was made entirely of wood and its various parts were bound together with wet rawhide, which became as hard as iron when it dried. The wheels were dish-shaped so that their broad rims did not cut deeply into the soil. Resting on the axle was a box in which the goods to be transported were carried. The cart could be used as a barge when rivers had to be crossed simply by removing the wheels, attaching them under the axle and box, and encasing everything in buffalo skins so that it floated like a raft.

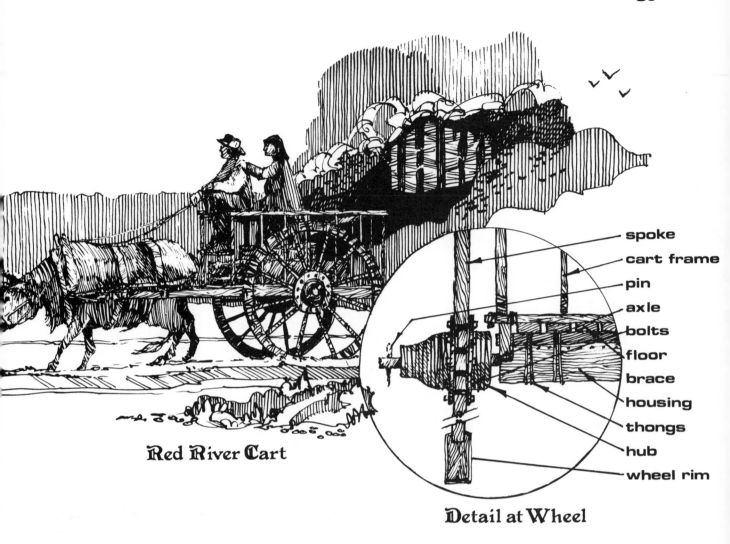

spoke
cart frame
pin
axle
bolts
floor
brace
housing
thongs
hub
wheel rim

Red River Cart

Detail at Wheel

The cart carried a load of about one thousand pounds and this weight could be pulled by oxen for a distance of twenty miles in a day. Being entirely made from such readily obtained materials as rawhide and wood, it was easily repaired, but tremendously noisy. Wood rubbing on wood is unpleasant at the best of times; it became deafening when a thousand wooden carts rumbled over the prairie together. The Métis learned to live with the noise, and their caravans cut trails across the prairies that can still be found today. Many of our major highways have been built on old Red River cart trails.

The First Rebellion, Red River 1869: an Apparent Victory

By the mid-1800s the Métis began to organize politically to secure their place in the growing country. They wanted a government in the northwest in which they could have some say, for they were ruled by governors in Ottawa and London whom they never saw and by fur company officials who feared the Métis' growing numbers.

The Métis sent many letters and petitions to the Canadian government in Ottawa asking to be represented and requesting deeds for the land that they claimed. They feared that the land, which was being mapped by government surveyors, would be given to settlers from the east.

On 11 October 1869, near St. Norbert in what is now Manitoba, a party of Métis led by Louis Riel prevented surveyors from mapping the land. The Métis argued that the northwest tradition, "He who occupies and uses the land is the owner," meant that the land was theirs.

Louis Riel was a leader of the Métis Council. Born near St. Boniface, Manitoba, on 22 October 1844, he had been educated at Red River and in Quebec and was respected as a deeply religious man.

When William McDougall, the newly appointed Lieutenant-Governor for the west, attempted to enter the area at Fort Pembina, an armed group of

Louis Riel

Métis Horsemen at Fort Pembina

Métis horsemen forced him to retreat to the
American side of the border. Fort Garry — now
Winnipeg — was seized on 1 November 1869 by the
Métis. Riel was elected president of the Métis
Council in January 1870 and delegates were sent to
the government in Ottawa to try to settle the Métis
land claims and to win the following rights:

A legislature of elected Métis.

Representation in the Canadian parliament.

The vote for every man over twenty-one years of
age.

The use of both French and English in courts and
local government.

Land for schools and roads.

A railway to Winnipeg, which had not yet been
scheduled as a railway stop.

A steamship service between Lake Superior and
the Red River.

Confirmation of Métis privileges and customs.

A few white settlers lived among the Métis and they too feared for their land when the surveyors arrived. But some whites did not agree with the Métis Council's demands to Ottawa, and one of these, a militant Protestant named Thomas Scott, was executed by the Métis. This incident caused trouble with the federal government.

As a result of the Métis delegation to Ottawa the province of Manitoba was created on 12 May 1870. The dream of the Métis to be part of the Confederation of Canada with their own elected government seemed to have been realized. The Métis, who made merry on all holy days and any other suitable occasion, celebrated, but it was not long before they realized that they had not won a clear victory. Soldiers arrived from Ontario, sent by the government to maintain law and order. Some of the soldiers were Swiss mercenaries and the others were Canadian volunteers, many of whom were not trained soldiers but men looking for excitement, or for revenge for the killing of Thomas Scott.

The Canadian government expelled Riel from Canada for five years for leading what they called a rebellion, and he went to live in the United States. The Métis showed that they supported Riel by electing him to the Parliament of Canada even though he was not allowed in Ottawa to take his seat. The other Métis leaders were assassinated or savagely beaten, often by the Canadian soldiers. The Métis suffered many humiliations, yet too often their attackers were not prosecuted by the authorities for fear of creating more trouble. Some of the Métis escaped violence by moving to the United States.

Métis Scrips

It was a bad time for those who stayed in Manitoba to take the land promised them at the time of Confederation. The land grants were slow in coming or badly administered, so confusion and further hardships resulted. Métis who had begun building homes on their land suddenly had their property taken from them and given to white immigrants who were pouring into the area.

Many of the Métis despaired of ever getting the land grants settled and gave up, selling their paper claims — scrips, they were called — to the land speculators who followed them everywhere. Many of them never even bothered to claim but moved farther west into what is now Alberta and Saskatchewan.

The Second Rebellion, Saskatchewan 1885 : Defeat

For a few years the Métis who moved west were able to pursue their old life. They built homes on the banks of the Saskatchewan rivers, planted gardens, and hunted buffalo. However, the millions of buffalo that once covered the prairie were almost gone and to find a herd, even a small one, was very difficult. The steamship and the railroad brought more immigrants, and by 1884 surveyors again appeared in their midst.

The Métis Council of Saskatchewan, headed by Gabriel Dumont, sent petitions and letters to Ottawa again to resolve land claims. The white settlers already there faced the same threat of the loss of their land, and supported the petitions. Ottawa ignored them.

Dumont, though a great leader, could neither read nor write. He knew that his people needed someone with a good education, someone who also understood their legal and political problems, to speak for them. The Council decided that Louis Riel be asked to return from exile, and Dumont and three councillors rode to Montana and persuaded him to come back. There was no new frontier to move to, and to obtain justice the Métis were prepared to die.

They sent word to Ottawa that they would prevent, by armed force if necessary, the surveying of land already claimed by Métis or white settlers. Ottawa responded by sending to Saskatchewan an army of Canadian volunteers, commanded by General Middleton, to put down this threatened rebellion.

Gabriel Dumont

The Métis made their stand against General Middleton and his troops in a little settlement called Batoche on the South Saskatchewan River on 9 May 1885. They were defeated.

Riel was executed in Regina for treason, and Gabriel Dumont escaped to the United States, where he lived for several years. Land claims were settled for only a few of the Métis.

Some say that Riel was a lunatic or a criminal, but to his people, he was their elected leader. He tried to lead them into a future which would guarantee them their lands, their dignity and their rights as a free people.

The Battle at Batoche

Epilogue

Today, the descendants of Riel's people make their homes in small towns and in big cities. Times have changed for them in the past hundred years, as for everyone. They are now better educated and have more understanding of their legal and political problems. They still seek fair land settlements from the Canadian government.

History calls them a defeated people, but the Métis do not feel defeated, and that is what is important. Today, as in the old days, they play their fiddles, sing, dance, and tell their children the old stories. They work hard, as they have always done. They do not mind when they are called Métis, halfbreeds, mixed bloods, Canadians or bois-brûles. They know who they are: "Ka tip aim soot chic" — the people who own themselves.